072266

Thayer, Marjorie
    The April foolers : a
play.

4C

The April Foolers

The April Foolers

A Play

By Marjorie Thayer
Pictures by Don Freeman

A
Golden
Gate
Junior
Book

Childrens
Press
•
Chicago

For Maggie

85138424

Library of Congress Cataloging in Publication Data

Thayer, Marjorie.
  The April foolers.

  "A Golden Gate junior book."
  SUMMARY: In their attempt to play a practical joke
on April Fools' Day, a group of children become the
victims themselves.
  1. April Fools' Day—Juvenile drama. 2. Practical
jokes—Juvenile drama. [1. April Fools' Day—Drama.
2. Plays] I. Freeman, Don. II. Title.
PN6120.A5T387   812'.5'4   77-15958
ISBN 0-516-08883-1

Characters

Randy

Pam

Bill

Nancy

Richard

Janie

Johnny

Mrs. Benton

ACT I
A quiet street in a small town

Early afternoon of April Fools' Day

Curtain rises

A group of children are huddled on the sidewalk. One of them is tying a black string to an old black handbag.

RANDY: You're not tying the string tight enough, Pam. It's going to come loose when I pull it.

PAM: It is not. Anyway, Mr. Smarty, who says *you're* going to pull it?

RANDY: *I* say so. On account of I thought of it for April Fools' Day last year.

RICHARD: You did not! We've played that dumb trick every April Fools' for years and years.

NANCY: That's the trouble. We've done it so long nobody ever falls for it any more.

BILL: Some people do. Maybe we'll catch somebody this time.

JANIE: I forget how we do it.

PAM: Don't you remember? We put the purse with the string on it right in the middle of the sidewalk. Then somebody comes along and sees it lying there— but they don't see the string, see. They think there's a lot of money in the purse and they lean over to grab it. (*Starts to laugh.*) When they're already to snatch, we pull it away and holler "April Fool!"

NANCY: Hey, get ready! Somebody's coming.

8

(Pam quickly places the purse on the sidewalk. Randy holds the string. The children rush out of sight. Enter Mrs. Benton. She glances at the purse, then walks on.)

MRS. BENTON *(over her shoulder):* April Fool, you kids! *(She exits.)*

(The children come out of hiding, looking disappointed.)

RANDY: Heck! She caught on right away.

NANCY: I told you that trick's so old nobody's going to fall for it.

JANIE: I wish somebody would, just once. I'd sure like to see it come off.

BILL: I bet I know somebody we can fool.

RANDY: Who?

BILL: Old Johnny. That kid's dumb enough to fall for anything.

RANDY: Yeah, you're right.

RICHARD: Old John's sure not very sharp. He probably hasn't even heard of April Fools' Day.

PAM: I guess kids don't learn very much when they grow up out in the country. Maybe he didn't even know when it was Christmas, ha-ha.

NANCY: I don't think Johnny's so dumb. It's just he hasn't lived in town very long.

9

BILL: Maybe we can find out how dumb he really is with the old purse trick.

PAM: He ought to be along here pretty soon. On his way home from that violin lesson his mother makes him take.

RANDY: Yeah, poor guy. But I sure wish we could think of a better joke to play on him. I'm tired of the old purse gag even if he does fall for it.

JANIE: We can give him some of the soap candy we made. He'll bite on *that.* (*She produces a paper bag and fishes out a square of soap candy.*)

RANDY: Oh, we've done that to everybody. I mean a real super-duper-extra-special April Fool trick.

JANIE: Like what?

RANDY: Well, let me think...

PAM: *I* know! Hey, you kids, how would you like to play a real good trick on old Johnny *and* Mrs. Benton?

NANCY: On Johnny *and* Mrs. Benton? You mean at the same time?

PAM: Sure. We could tell John that Mrs. Benton's giving a party tonight and he's invited. Mrs. Benton wants he should be guest of honor! We'll tell Johnny to get all dressed up and go over to Mrs. Benton's at six o'clock. Then, when Mrs. Benton comes to the door, she'll tell him there *isn't* any party.

RICHARD (*excited*): All of us could be hiding in the bushes by her front porch. When Mrs. Benton tells Johnny there isn't going to be any party we'll jump out and holler "April Fool!"

BILL: And then we'll run like anything!

JANIE: Mrs. Benton's sure going to be mad when she finds out we're only playing an old April Fool joke. She might even call the police or something.

NANCY: Oh, that would be terrible! My mother wouldn't like *that*.

BILL: *I* know! All of us have to wear a disguise! Like the bad guys on TV. Then Mrs. Benton won't catch on it's us.

RANDY: That's a great idea—but like what? We haven't got very much time to make disguises…

RICHARD: We could make masks out of paper bags to wear over our heads—like we did at Halloween. Then *nobody* would know it's us!

PAM: My mom has dozens and dozens of great big paper bags. She saves them every time she comes home from the market. She'll never miss 'em if we swipe a few.

RANDY: Listen, you guys. After we tell old Johnny about the party tonight we'll go over to Pam's house and make some terrific masks. Nobody—but *nobody*—will ever know who we are!

JANIE: *(looking down the block):* Hey, here comes Johnny! Don't say anything, anybody, about April Fools' or he might catch on. Pam, you tell him about Mrs. Benton's party.

(Enter Johnny, carrying a violin case.)

CHILDREN *(together)*: Hi, John…Hello, Johnny…How are you doing, John?

JOHNNY *(a little surprised):* Hi, everybody. I'm okay I guess. How're you all?

RANDY: Hey, John, have we got news for you!

BILL: Yea, man!

PAM: I mean *good* news!

JOHNNY: Okay, what is it? I sure could use some good news.

PAM: Well, you know Mrs. Benton, don't you? That nice lady who lives in the big house next to the church?

JOHNNY: Mrs. Benton? Yeah, I guess. I know who she is all right.

PAM: Well, she's giving a party tonight and she *specially* wants *you* to come! She told us to be *sure* and invite you.

JOHNNY: How come? I don't hardly even know her. How come she's asking me to a party?

JANIE: Well, I guess she likes you. 'Cause she sure wants you to come. Maybe it's because you're new around here.

JOHNNY: That's pretty crazy. Are the rest of you going?

NANCY: *(trying not to giggle):* Oh sure! We'll be there.

JANIE: We wouldn't miss it for the world!

JOHNNY: Well, what time?

RANDY: Six o'clock tonight. And be sure you're on time.

PAM: And dress up—in your very best suit.

JOHNNY *(doubtfully)*: Well, I don't know. I don't dress up very often…But I guess I could wear that white shirt and the tie my mom makes me wear on Sundays.

CHILDREN *(together)*: Neat!…That'll be swell…You'll look terrific…Atta boy, John!

JOHNNY *(shyly)*: Gosh, I've hardly ever been to a real party…

PAM: Well, don't be late. Mrs. Benton wouldn't like it if you were late. Remember—the party's at six. On the dot, like we told you.

JOHNNY: You guys are *sure* you'll be there?

RANDY: Yeah, we told you. But don't wait for any of us. As soon as you get there just walk right up and ring the doorbell.

JOHNNY: Oh, I won't wait for you. And I'll be on time all right…

Curtain

ACT II

Scene I:
The same street, a little while later. The children are gone and the sidewalk is empty.

Curtain rises

(Enter Mrs. Benton. She has been to the market and is carrying a large bag of groceries. Enter Johnny from the opposite side.)

MRS. BENTON: Well, hello, Johnny. How have you been? I haven't seen you lately.

JOHNNY: Hi, Mrs. Benton. I guess I'm fine. Hey, Mrs. Benton, do you want I should help you carry those groceries? They look pretty heavy.

MRS. BENTON: Why, thank you, Johnny, but I think I can manage.

JOHNNY: I sure wouldn't mind carrying them for you, Mrs. Benton. I guess they're probably things for the party.

MRS. BENTON *(puzzled)*: The party?

JOHNNY: I mean for the party tonight. It was sure swell of you to invite me, Mrs. Benton. I already told my mother and she said it was okay for me to come.

MRS. BENTON *(setting down the groceries on the sidewalk)*: She did! Well! Who told you about the party, Johnny?

JOHNNY: Oh, Randy and Pam and Richard and all the other kids. I was sure surprised when they said you wanted me to come. Nobody's ever invited me to a real party before. It was real nice of you to ask me, Mrs. Benton.

MRS. BENTON: Did the children tell you what time to come, Johnny?

JOHNNY: They said to be at your house at six o'clock—and not to be late. I plan to be right on time!

MRS. BENTON: Did Randy and the others say they'd be there at six too?

JOHNNY: Oh, yes. None of us want to be late, I guess.

MRS. BENTON: Johnny, do you know what day this is?

JOHNNY (*surprised*): Why, it's Friday.

MRS. BENTON: Yes, of course it is. But I mean, do you know the *date*?

JOHNNY: Well, I guess I don't, Mrs. Benton. I guess I don't keep very good track
  of things like that.

MRS. BENTON: That's all right, John. I just wanted to know if you knew.

JOHNNY (*anxiously*): Is everything all right, Mrs. Benton? I mean, you *want* I should come tonight, don't you?

MRS. BENTON (*making up her mind*): Of course I do, Johnny! You come right along at six o'clock. We're going to have the best party you ever heard of! We'll have games and stunts and lots and lots of good things to eat.

JOHNNY: Gosh, that sounds swell!

MRS. BENTON: By the way, if you happen to see any of the other children between now and time for the party, I think you'd better not say anything about our little talk. We'll just keep the party plans a secret between you and me.

JOHNNY: Oh, sure, Mrs. Benton. I won't say a word. I know you're going to be planning lots of surprises...

MRS. BENTON: You're so right, Johnny, you're so right. In fact, I know a number of boys and girls who are going to get the surprise of their lives!

Curtain

Curtain rises

Scene II: *The front of Mrs. Benton's house, a few minutes before six o'clock.*
Enter Randy, Pam, Richard, Janie, Bill and Nancy.

RANDY (*in a low voice*): Don't make any noise, you guys. Just hide in those bushes.

RICHARD: What'll we do if Johnny doesn't show up?

PAM: He'll show all right.

RANDY: Sure he will. Now don't forget. Wait till he rings the doorbell and Mrs. Benton comes to the door. We have to give her time to tell him there isn't any party.

PAM: Don't yell "April Fool" until she's told him!

BILL: Then—get out of here *fast!* Mrs. Benton's going to be real mad. (*Janie and Nancy begin to giggle.*)

RANDY: *Sh-h-h,* everybody! Pipe down. Do you want to spoil the trick?

JANIE: We sure don't. It's the best April Fools' joke we ever played.

RANDY: Well, then, pipe down and get behind those bushes.

JANIE: Okay, okay. (*She crawls into the bushes.*) Nobody can see *me.*

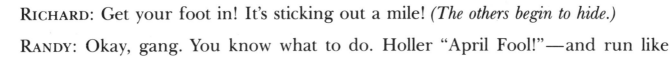

RICHARD: Get your foot in! It's sticking out a mile! *(The others begin to hide.)*

RANDY: Okay, gang. You know what to do. Holler "April Fool!"—and run like crazy! *(He disappears behind a bush.)*

(Enter Johnny. He hesitates a moment, then walks up to the front door and rings the door-bell. Almost at once the door is opened by Mrs. Benton. Music is heard in the background.)

MRS. BENTON: Good evening, Johnny. *(Raising her voice a little)* I'm so glad you could come to the party. Come right in.

JOHNNY: Hi, Mrs. Benton. I'm sure glad I could come too. *(He walks through the door which Mrs. Benton closes behind him. A short pause, then the April Fool pranksters come out, one by one. They gather a safe distance from the front porch.)*

PAM: I don't believe it! She really *is* giving a party!

RICHARD: And she never invited *us!*

NANCY: That's *mean!* How could she be so *mean?*

RANDY: I don't get it. We made up a party for an April Fools' trick—and now there really *is* a party! How come?

PAM: I don't know how come. But it sure is terrible to be left out!

(*Johnny appears in the window. He is eating a large dish of ice cream.*)

NANCY: I can't stand it! Let's get out of here!

JANIE: This is the worst April Fools' I ever remember!

RANDY: I guess the joke's on us all right. *Let's go!*

(As they start to leave Mrs. Benton opens the front door.)

MRS. BENTON: Don't go away—Pam, Randy and the rest of you. You can take off those masks now. (*The children remove the paper bags.*)

PAM: I guess we have to go home now, Mrs. Benton.

MRS. BENTON: This won't take long, Pam. I think you children are wondering about the party inside, aren't you?

PAM: Well, yes—I guess we are, Mrs. Benton.

MRS. BENTON: When you invited Johnny to my house tonight you thought there wasn't going to be a party, didn't you? You just made it up. That's right, isn't it?

RANDY: We only wanted to play an April Fools' joke on Johnny, Mrs. Benton.

MRS. BENTON: And you never stopped to think how Johnny would feel when he found out the party was only a trick?

PAM: But—I guess we don't understand, Mrs. Benton. On account of you really *are* giving a party.

28

MRS. BENTON: I hadn't *planned* a party until I happened to meet Johnny this afternoon and he told me what you had told him. Then I realized how very cruel it would be to disappoint him. You see, he really believed every word you said.

NANCY: Gosh, Mrs. Benton—we didn't mean to be cruel to Johnny.

JANIE: We didn't even think about it...

MRS. BENTON: That's just the trouble—you didn't think. Children, it's time you learned the difference between a cruel joke and a funny one. You see, Johnny didn't even know it was April Fools' Day. That means your joke wasn't funny at all, doesn't it?

CHILDREN *(together)*: We sure are sorry, Mrs. Benton...We're really-truly sorry ...We sure are...

MRS. BENTON: I think you know now how it feels to be on the other end of a joke.

RANDY: You mean—the party is a joke on us? On account of we're not invited?

MRS. BENTON: Yes, that's just what I mean. Children, do you truly think you deserve to come to a party?

PAM: Well—no, I guess not.

RICHARD: I guess we don't. I guess we sure know now how it feels to be disappointed. *(The children turn away, starting to leave.)*

MRS. BENTON: Wait a minute, everybody. *Johnny* is the one who is going to be disappointed if you're not here. And *I* think you have learned a great big lesson on April Fools' Day. So come on in—there's plenty of ice cream for everybody. Johnny *(calling over her shoulder)*, your friends are here!

(The children are happily crowding through the front door as the curtain falls.)

It was April Fool's Day again but this year the children were both disappointed and bored. No one had fallen for any of the April Fool tricks they had so carefully planned. For instance, Mrs. Benton had walked right by the empty purse with its hidden string which they had planted in the middle of the sidewalk. So discouraged were they that they were sure that even Johnny, new boy in town and thus their most likely target, wouldn't even bite on the soap candy. What was needed, they decided, was something new—a real "super-duper-extra-special April Fool trick." It was Pam who came up with the Super Idea—a way to fool both Johnny *and* Mrs. Benton at one and the same time. The trick was amusing enough, except to its intended victims. How Mrs. Benton managed to turn it around and to show its perpetrators the difference between a cruel joke and a funny one provide an unexpected climax to a play children will love to produce and also to read. Don Freeman's engaging illustrations in full color are a treat in themselves.

MARJORIE THAYER is the author of three previous plays, *The First Day of School, The Valentine Box* and *The Halloween Witch*. She has also written a Christmas story, *The Christmas Strangers*, illustrated by Don Freeman and published by Childrens Press in 1976. A native Californian, Miss Thayer is a graduate of the University of California at Berkeley. She has been an editor of children's books, in both New York and California, for many years. She now makes her home in Hollywood.

DON FREEMAN'S many books have earned him a very special place in the hearts of children everywhere. Beginning with his first successes, *Chuggy And The Blue Caboose* and *Pet Of The Met,* he has continued to write and illustrate a wide variety of such charming tales as *Corduroy* and *A Pocket For Corduroy, Quiet! There's A Canary In The Library, Flash The Dash, Will's Quill* and other titles too numerous to mention. Born in San Diego, California, Mr. Freeman spent many years in New York where, among other occupations, he was a newspaper artist for the New York *Times* and New York *Herald Tribune.* He now makes his home in Santa Barbara.